Your attempt to enjoy these poems is considered unsatisfactory

A collection by Gary From Leeds

No part of this book may be reproduced or transmitted in any manner without written permission from Listen Softly London, or the author, except in the case of brief quotations embodied in critical articles or reviews. All rights reserved.

Listen Softly London
333 Muswell Hill Broadway
London
N10 1BY

ListenSoftlyLondon.com
@ListenSoftlyLDN

Your attempt to enjoy these poems is considered unsatisfactory
COPYRIGHT © 2016 by Gary Hartley
First Edition, May 2016
Cover Design by Aaron Lipschitz
Edited by Dominic Stevenson
Typeset by Aaron Lipschitz

ISBN: 978-0-9935353-2-1

Published in the United Kingdom

Gary From Leeds is also known as Gary Hartley, Gary W. Hartley, Son and Brother but never ever Gaz or, worse still, Gareth.

Thanks to:

Chris Boyd for the mouthwash.
Everyone else who thinks they deserve one.

Contents

0. UP & AT 'EM

Disclaimer For An Unwritten Poem	8
Your Attempt To Enjoy This Poem is Considered Unsatisfactory	10

1. PEOPLE & PLACES

Freud's Only Knock Knock Joke	12
Dated	13
Wednesday, Early Evening	14
The New English Hymnal	15
Person Under A Train	17
Entente Cordiale	18
Lorry on a narrow road	20
The limits of free speech	22
Civil service development programme	23
A Camden Venue	24
Leaving Leeds Coach Station	25
Nails	26
British Waterways	27
Love letter to a public park	28
Kingdom in exile	30
Conspiracy '04	32

2. CONCEPTS AND THEORIES

Up'ncoming	34

Old Conservative's Final Haiku	35
Enter The Void	36
Whitehall Art School Degree Show	37
Pessimist's Anthem	39
Show Off	41
Observational Haiku	42
Strangers in a Home	43
Heimlich Manoeuvre	44
Pain/Relief	45

3. FOOD & DRINK

Life Advice With Cheese	47
Spoiled Sweets	49
Self-destructive poem	50
Meal	51
Picking at Craft Beer Labels	53
Anxiety in the Womad Green Room	55
Utilitarian Haiku	56
An Easy Mistake to Make	57

4. SPORT & LEISURE

Detail	59
Do as Diouf	60
Field Day	61
Facial	62
Work in Progress	63
Bear Gryllis	65

Dead Space Decoration	66
Man and Sunbed	67
Street Soccer Tactics	68
Art/House	70
Zeroes	71
The Bitter and Twisted Tale of Phil Masinga	73
Sanctions of the FIFA Ethical Committee	76
WC1/EC1	77

5. ODDS & SODS

Repeat Offender	79
Deep Cuts	81
Guess Who's	82
Not Bitter	83
Perpetual Winter	84
Raspberry Beret	85
Apathaiku	86
The Consultant' Consultant	87
Casio MT-20	89
No opening	90
Gold, Frankincense and That	92
Going Out	93
Left Untitled	94
Vision of the Future	95
Poetic Potential	96

0. UP & AT 'EM

Disclaimer For An Unwritten Poem

    i.   The opinions expressed in this poem
Are those of the author
Definitely not their employer
And in the case of controversy
Possibly not really even the author
    ii.   All the disclaims in this disclaimer
Apply to this disclaimer itself
As well as the poem that does not
Follow this disclaimer
    iii.   Any line marked with an asterisk
Is a line brought to you
In partnership with a commercial sponsor
Washing machines last longer with Calgon
Asterisk
Or else the asterisk is possibly
Just there for aesthetic effect
    iv.   No possibles or other uncertainties
Will be clarified at any point in this poem
    v.   This poem abides by the standards
Laid down by the Arts Council
Medical Research Council and
Leeds City Council
    vi.   This poem is suitable for all age groups
Though parents with children under 12
May choose to seek independent advice
    vii.   This poem is both arty and farty but
Not affiliated to any political party
    viii.   This poem was conceived at the University of Life
But also went to an actual university

Your attempt to enjoy these poems is considered unsatisfactory

    ix.   This poem has been scientifically
Proven to be emotionally intelligent
With some anecdotal evidence suggesting
It is also actually intelligent
    x.   This poem can do a rubix cube
In less than a minute and
Fit a light bulb in similar
    xi.   This poem will not rely on stereotypes
Except when they're true
    xii.   This poem will not be used as
Evidence in a court of law or
A filling station forecourt
    xiii.   This poem will now not begin.

Your Attempt To Enjoy This Poem is Considered Unsatisfactory

If you're not feeling this poem
it's because you're not ethically aware –
in fact you're entirely morally bankrupt
like someone who reads the
FT's *How to Spend It* supplement.
If you're not feeling this poem
your ears are on wonky –
full of wax or not properly
tuned to the dimension that
this poem chooses to operate in.
If you're not feeling this poem
it's because it's gone over your head.
You're an idiot.
A moron, a sickpot and a twit.
Or it could be just that it's shit

1. PEOPLE & PLACES

Freud's Only Knock Knock Joke

Knock knock
Who's there?
Yer mum.

Dated

I am alive — you are dead.
Not sure how you managed
to register with Match.com
in the first place.
But now we're here
we might as well crack on.
So…what do you do for a living?
Oh shit—not sure living is the best
place to start.

Wednesday, Early Evening

What do you mean the offer's not available?
Just because I'm here with no-one else
doesn't mean I'm not entitled to my two-for-one tickets.
Someone needs to take a stand against this world –
marketed at tedious twosomes, pairs and duos.
I need that extra seat – was going to do a jigsaw on it.
Hand them over or things will get pretty nasty round here.

The guy on the other till did try and get a word in, but those things did:
A samurai sword appeared at speed out of a concealed pocket;
Odeon cinema representative swiftly beheaded;
Head rolling beside a promotional cardboard cut-out of Ryan Gosling.

I didn't have to do this, it could've been so different if he'd just
shown a little, a little flexibility, less jobs worth.
But Sir – what I was trying to say is it's actually
Thursday.
And the promotion's ended anyway.

The New English Hymnal

clickety – clack
clickety – clack
interchangeable
office drag and drop
with rail journeys
to nowhere
god life's boring
holidays to
interval monotony
sometimes pop
or popcorn
accompaniment
options to ponder
in the break
an occasional
aperitif
to dive or drown in
god life's boring
shifting occasionally
often to
more than occasional
aperitifs
and you're
getting the bends
over backwards
once more again
write it up
to be read by no-one
bloggedy blog
amazing

yeah, fucking amazing
the next best
box set
might learn
animal husbandry
or get laser treatment
for the short sight
not letting the cracks show
papering skills
bordering on origami
eating five a day
so healthy
etcetera etcetera
Amen.

Person Under A Train

For once it wasn't a euphemism.
They just crawled underneath
when it came to a halt

And now they're taunting
the station staff
who are armed with brooms.

Entente Cordiale

Sometimes
France and I sit down
over a leisurely café au lait
and reminisce about
the good old days
the golden age of enmity
Generals spouting about territory
you and me
me and you
Staring across water
bliss

Now there are too many
Enemies to know properly:
Asylum seekers
Benefits cheaters
Terrorists
Tax evaders
Journalists
Internet perverts
Gypsies with blonde kids
Celebrities on social networks
The enemy within
whoever they are

All in all, bloody exhausting
It's not even clear
If we should be fighting
Or just chatting some
Outraged shit

About freedom
Then helping some others
do the nasty business
while we sip flat whites
with strangers
in the deserted car parks
of out-of-town shopping malls

The caffeine kicks
but makes no contact
and France and I say:
Come; let's do it
let's play British Bulldogs
on the English Channel
Wear bright colours
for sporting chances
fire cannons, giggling madly
As if this simple kind of
hatred could have
gone on forever.

Lorry on a narrow road

You're a wanker, he said.
I can't get through there, he said.
What do you think this is? He said.
You're a wanker, he said.

He's a wanker, he said.
Expecting support from
pavement rubber-neckers
on the issue of
whether the driver of
the minibus was a regular
masturbator or not.

Have you seen the space
he's leaving me?
He's a wanker, he said.

You're a wanker, he said.
A superfluous affectation
as the minibus was now reversing

Having nervously unloaded
its cargo of
primary school children

Undeterred
he threw in a finger
from a wound-down window
at the point of passing

Some people are so rude, he said.
As the drama began to recede
and normality resume
before adding in crescendo:
What a fucking wanker.

The limits of free speech

In the giddy headrush
that comes

with calling
absolutely everyone cunts

they had neglected
to conclude

that they themselves
were one

Civil service development programme

The muddled bureaucrat
sits quieter at desk than
usual

No-one asks why since
Outlook's still open

But the muddled bureaucrat
is definitely quieter than
usual

In fact the muddled bureaucrat
is dead.

A Camden Venue

The Little Boys' Room seemingly has got bigger,
taken over the whole dance floor in fact.
The cocks swing as if dancing with urinals strapped to belts
crossing your legs, ashamed of your own.

And these, apparently the respectable ones.
Not like those butchers of the West End meat market
but easy to see the game's long commuted here
ambitions of fellatio-feeding on the rotting carcass of indie.

You better come equipped with umbrella, girls, women, femmes
on this Camden crawl through desperation's annals,
in all likelihood you'll get soaked with spit and pre-club spunk.
And they'll still ask if it hurt when you fell from heaven

Leaving Leeds Coach Station

Uncertain rewards
Fucking rife here.
Britney's Nails
Next to Mecca Bingo.
Flat cap man
Surrounded by
Carrier bags
Pumps his heart
Into an accordion.
The queue at station
Greggs is massive.

Nails

When he came down south
he kept himself alert at all times.
He knew to look out for hard men
prowling hard the hard streets
bludgeoning flesh like his for laughs
with hardly any invite at all.
He'd seen *Lock Stock* you see…

But after an incident-free while
he started to think,
he had the measure of the hard men.
And just when he'd let his guard down
the hard water beat him to death.

British Waterways

Lovely for dog walking.
Bloated dead dog, floating.

Ducks and ducklings swim by.
Nest of scrap metal.

Thriving flora.
Japanese Knotweed
annihilates local gardens.

Cruising gracefully.
Unwatched kid drowns in lock.

Rare mammal spotted.
Concrete-landscaped
waterside development.

Idyllic life, bobbing gently.
Jogger murdered at dusk.

Peace and quiet.
Man in mac, wanking.

Love letter to a public park

Been warned off you, Burgess Park.

Told you're a
bad influence
Particularly after
dark.

That your name
has that ring about it.

Of unsolved brutal
crime, disaster.

Like Hatfield and rail crashes

but I like to
jog there in that
moody personal space
of yours

I can see the blue sky
only here:
Night-blue.
Not that sold-out
Day version blue
we're forced
to share our love under.

And if I die
in Burgess Park

indulging this love affair
then at least folks reading
the news will say ah…
That's irony for sure.

Not the Alanis Morrisette
rain on your wedding day version

But the hard stuff.

Kingdom in exile

It takes 2,467 160-bag
boxes of Yorkshire Tea
to build a liveable bungalow.

Not a lot of people know that.

But it's vital information
if you're building a microcosm
of God's own county

Far enough away from God's own county
to mean no building
methodology is gonna make
you appear any more silly

That crunch underfoot
as you walk to the door,
it's Henderson's Relish
flavoured Yorkshire Crisps.

Pricier than gravel, certainly,
but few would argue less tasty
as a footpath garnish

All this to fill a void:
No one's repping at street level
since Woolworths folded.

No Yorkshire exile's got
anything to touch.

You can't feel the texture
of Good Honest Broadband

You can't write a Yorkshire cheque,
or be paid in Yorkshire currency,
since National Australia
bought out Yorkshire Bank.

So I sit in my bath of
lukewarm tea
and floating soggy crisp crumbs
waiting for this to feel like home.

Conspiracy '04

We were both in a cheap hostel
in Stockholm, Sweden
when Shahin Mir Mohammed Hosseini
blurted out to an audience of
feckless inter-railers

That he was an exiled political poet
with abnormal teeth and sleep problems.

Abnormal teeth due to radio transmitters
implanted thereby Iranian spies

Sleep problems due to said spies
inconsiderately choosing to time
their hostile communications
for when he's tucked up in bed

He handed out a grammatically suspect
print-out complete with diagrams to prove as much,
but volunteered no poems
published in a reputable journal
or otherwise.

It may have been because of the latter
that I didn't believe him.

And still don't.

2. CONCEPTS AND THEORIES

Up'ncoming

First comes art
Then comes cafés
Then comes office couples who lobby for a Waitrose
Then goes art
To somewhere with an Aldi

Old Conservative's Final Haiku

When M&S Foods
Accept need for value range
Aspiration dies

Enter The Void

Have you known true emptiness?
Have you faced down the abyss?

Have you fallen into a
pitch-black swirling vortex
of never-ending
unimaginable horror?

I have done all these things,

for I, on more than one occasion

have looked into the eyes
of a recruitment consultant.

Whitehall Art School Degree Show

The Home Office
is making a movie
from all the reels
of CCTV film.
The edit suite,
a fucking nightmare.

The Department for Education
is working on a
conceptual piece
about the enthusiasm of youth
versus the drive to achievement.

The Department of Energy
is singing the last song
of long-dead beasts
archived underground.

The Department for International Development
is watching itself
reflected back
repeating old mistakes
performance art.

The Department for Environment, Food and Rural Affairs
is starving itself to
fuel the creative process
capturing the results in
analogue, monochrome.

The Department for Work and Pensions
graduated last year
after a spell in a call centre
has been allowed to regress
work as yet unsubmitted.

The Department for Justice
sensory deprivation
in a tank of formaldehyde.

The Cabinet Office
just a cabinet
Installation piece.

The Treasury
never off the phone to dealers
though hasn't yet started
to create.

The Department for Culture
has been caught napping
with its pants down
and is trying to sell it all
as slapstick.

Pessimist's Anthem

Quit
Just quit
Just quit
Just quit.
Quit while you're ahead
Quit while you're behind
Quit this
Quit that
Quit the other.
Especially the other.
Quit smoking
Quit not smoking
Get jobs
just so you can quit them
Quit present tense
and all the others
Quit things you haven't
even started yet
Go back in time
and quit history.
Quit respiration
Quit contemplation
Quit being quick witted
Quit telling people to quit
Quit watching
Quit waiting
Quit hoping
Don't even start hoping,
In fact quit starting
stopping

procrastinating
and pausing for breath
Quit
Quit
Quit
Yes quit and quit and
Quit once more again
for good measure
Quit so much
and so damn profoundly
That no-one could
ever call you
A quitter.

Show Off

Bike exhibition
Cake exhibition
People who want to live in France exhibition
Baby exhibition
Boat exhibition
1950s revivalist exhibition
Grow your own exhibition
Career exhibition
Pyramid ponzi land-grab exhibition
War exhibition
Outdoor exhibition
How to look good naked exhibition
Dog, cat, goat exhibition
Life, death, god exhibition
Play your cards right
Get down Earls Court early
and you could make
An exhibition
of yourself.

Observational Haiku

Comedy success
Is mostly dependent on
Being called Russell

Strangers in a Home

Burglar don't like their Hitchcock.
Rifled through the box set
not one to their taste.

Vertigo's avoidance
predictable given
their ground-floor entry,

but judging by the scuff-marks
you'd have assumed an interest
in Rear Window at least.

They took a half-finished
bottle of Robinson's squash,
a bag of Haribo

but steered well clear
of *Frenzy, Rope*
and even *Psycho*.

Burglar don't like their Hitchcock.
Is this non-theft a critique?

An attack on the hackneyed dialogue
of *The Birds*
The overuse of concluding
action sequences in music halls,

or Alfred's output being
far sketchier generally than
self-described film-buffs attest,

or maybe it's just
a simple show of disapproval
at this 14-disc set's omission
of *North by Northwest*.

Gary From Leeds

Heimlich Manoeuvre

Do you think that more lives
would be saved
if it sounded less Germanic?

Pain/Relief

I'm a conceptualist
sado-masochist
pacifist.
Though abhorring
violence,
both giving and
receiving
Goddamn,
I like the idea
of it.

3. FOOD & DRINK

Life Advice With Cheese

Do good,
but don't be a do-gouda.

Be bold with your ideas,
Be a paneer.

Roquefort if you have to,
but avoid hundred years' wars

You'll never succeed at the circus
with just one stilton

Never read a gorgonzola
naturalism excites the snakes -

and never treat berkswell
they'll only throw it back at you.

Camembert! Crack out your chest,
it's ok to be hirsute, ignore the haters.

Experiment with chemicals.
but don't go emmenthal.

You may be the huntsman,
but be mindful of the hunted.

Don't dream of a red Leicester,
they play in blue and always will do.

Nor a red Windsor either.
Even more support for blue.

Stay well clear of stinking bishops,
and smelly elders of other godly gangs.

Visit remote places:
The Isle of Mull
Lincolnshire

You may be faced in rural climes,
with the occasional laughing cow
I say: laugh with them

and remember, you're Seriously Strong,
but you can Dairylea(n) on me when you're not.

Knowing all that,
life's a brie(z).

Spoiled Sweets

Well I suppose you can't have known
that the little bubbles in Aeros
are made from the last breaths of
dying orphans with terminal diseases.

The bubbles in Maltesers similar,
but with dying kitten breaths.

You maybe weren't aware
that the crunchy outer shell of
your M&Ms is just so due to a tiny
pinch of Osprey egg shell.

Poached illegally before hatching
of course

You simply can't have seen the evidence
that the curls in a Curly Wurly
are produced by hand
via forced child labour in sweatshops
and detainees in Guantanamo

And for god's sake don't
get me started on Jelly Babies.

Self-destructive poem

Paracetamol
Paracetamol
I've only gone
And etamol

<u>Meal</u>

mouth wash required
striving to be the
most influential arse-licker.

some kind of regression
to the mean, and
yes it is mean.

a relentless chase
round the dinner table

for compliments from
people with intangible
qualities.

nothing rare or medium
possible here,
just overdone.

choking it down
amidst fake laughter
with no condiments.

the haters don't even
muster the art of hate
just reheated

twice-melted down
re-moulded
I Can't Believe it's Not
passion.

fruit cake genius
gets no stage time
to shine, but
we all say we're dining
well.

before
going to puke our guts up
out the back

Picking at Craft Beer Labels

It's such a wacky place!
it's like a bar
except not
except yeah
pretty much a bar
Bottled beer, staff, etcetera.

It's such a wacky place!
with music
except not
except yeah
pretty much music
DJ decks, speakers, etcetera.

It's such a wacky place!
With an industrial estate
vibe you know
paint peeling
off the walls
plastic seating
prices marked up
at authenticity's
current rate.

It's such a wacky place!
No.

It does not
cover the void
stop me contemplating
death

sitting alone in my pants
eating Carte D'or
from the tub but

it's only in stylised squalor and
overpriced booze
that I can find grace
so keep saying it's ace, please
it's ace man it's ace
it's such a wacky place.

Anxiety in the Womad Green Room

Does Toumani Diabate
eat pate?
Probably not, eh.
Does Salif Keita eat potata?
Does Lee 'Scratch' Perry
glug peri-peri
or prefer a rich dessert
based on cherry?
Has Gilberto Gil
had his fill?
Does Giles Peterson
want some fajitas on?
And how does Craig Charles
like his crack?

Utilitarian Haiku

Goggles made of beer
though useful sometimes, maybe
are shit for swimming

An Easy Mistake to Make

CCTV captured everything.

Turned out pistachio pieces
did not disguise features.

The cashier, unfazed,
licked my face.

Cops let me off
after having a go
at the remaining honey residue.

The day I tried to rob a bank
in a baklava.

4. SPORT & LEISURE

Detail

Air-hockey
Buckaroo
Canasta
Dominos
Elephant polo
Frustration
Golf
Hockey
Ice Hockey
Jumanji
Korfball
Lawn Tennis
Mousetrap
NBA Jam
Operation
Pop-up Pirate
Quasar
Risk
Solitaire
Tetris
Uno
Volleyball
World of Warcraft
Xiangqi
Yahtzee
Zelda…
Everyone says
you must play the game
No-one ever tells you
which one.

Do as Diouf

If we could just be a bit more like
El-Hadji Diouf,
life would be easier for all

No more passive-aggressive
email chains
that could imply
desire, or disgust,

No more sharpening
subtle knives for
later use

Let us learn from
the reviled man of
the beautiful game

A Senegalese
Sun Tzu, if you will

Zealously face the critics
revel in the role
of the Captain Hook
of the Panto

Leave the haters in
no doubt:
Spit in their face.

Field Day

Look at them all, like lice on a well-washed youth's head of hair.
No giant comb is handy for the good public's sanitation.
Height of expression the woolly hat worn high,
perhaps a parody of the ride a cap took on the skulls of East 17.
But this is one of many thoughts nowhere near interesting enough to be held longer than 1.5 seconds.

This day's to be spent in a field except it's not strictly a field but a whole park
and it's not strictly a day but a number of hours
Mock-casual laughs jitter but the looks exchanged are tense.
Do they look enough the same as everyone else to thrive?
If not, how much Magners and ketamine might be needed to fake it harder?
Hark the herald DJ collectives spin, hip hip hip hooray.
All hail the not-field not-day.

Facial

She decided to make,
and use,
toothbrushes
out of cuttings
from bearded
foreign men
at house parties.
Her teeth took
on a hue of
vague mystique,
and soon she
was talking about
Lars Von Trier
like she knew him.

Work in Progress

For Christmas
I want my own
Bus stop
countdown timer
So I can be constantly
waiting for
something or other.

People will
view my
future sitting down
as not just sitting down
anymore
but sitting down
with purpose.

You don't have to
wrap it up
It'll obviously be
a bus stop countdown
timer in there.

Plus surprise
is both redundant
and of little interest
to such a
newly-fledged
man with a plan.

As well as buses

And other transportation
I intend to utilise
I'll add to my glowing display:
future arguments
feelings
most future meals.

I might visit clairvoyants
to try and schedule
my death date
to a reasonable
level of accuracy

leave the odd slot free
for spontaneity

I want to carry
my bus stop
countdown timer
on my person at all times
with a portable stand
for show.

I want to emanate
patience,
steely resolve
LED-based
technological wizardry.

I want to give the
impression
I've got things to
look forward to.

Bear Gryllis

The difference between
liking the outdoors
and being outdoorsy

is for the latter to ring true
you have to enjoy
getting there.

Personally favouring
teleportation
to sites of natural beauty,

I am willing to give scientists
a few more years
to work on this

before investing in
decent walking shoes.

Dead Space Decoration

Deflated balloon
Skulking in the corner
of a house party kitchen.
Static picking up forgotten crumbs.
You talked to me once,
but now have found
Someone better

Man and Sunbed

He's got a tan
That football man
He's certainly more
Tanned
Than the average
White man

And 50-something
Mothers like that
Look

There was one
Just one
More theme of
Interest
About the
Tanned man
In a past life

As the nice
Guy of the game

With no career
Yellow cards
And significantly less
Of a bioluminescent glow

But with
The moral high
Ground
Long extinguished

The man
Has become
More or less
Just Melanin.

Street Soccer Tactics

Semi-stranger danger
you're not meant
to be here

You're a Monday night
5-a-side
football player

Your existence
is null
outside Astroturf

No kick-off time
scheduled

No advance payment
made for this
piece of pavement
at this moment

Though we both
look at our watches
frozen

Waiting for a
lucky quirk
in the space/time
continuum

We're mutually
spotted
undoubtedly
If this was

a set-piece
the pundits
would bemoan
the abject quality of
the marking

But should you move
towards me
or engage me
in any way

I will not hesitate
to slide tackle
in direct
contravention
of Powerleague rules

Because life,
fair acquaintance,
is not Powerleague

Something
you seem to have
failed to have
grasped

Please take this
awkward glancing at the
ground to mean

You too should probably
just pretend
not to exist
see you on Monday.
Mate.

Art/House

We would get out more
but our house is too nice.
Oh go on then,
to the theatre café.

The arts exist
to raise the market value
of coffee and cake.

To bake is the pragmatist's
to paint, *to* perform.

The arts exist
as a lobbying arm
of the residential
property industry.

As the spin doctors
turning garages
to live/work spaces

the arts exist
to make life difficult
for itself.
What arty pain! What arty angst!

Licking crumbs from crevices
of credit-crunch-resistors
Cry me a valuable river

Zeroes

It's still nil-nil lads
It's never not nil-nil here.

Captain call to arms
Though they've just smashed
their fifth in
against a rag-tag squadron
of misfiring misfits
who've never acquainted
barn door and banjo
in anger or any other state.

It's still nil-nil lads
goal number six
has just dribbled home
goalie lips quiver noticeably
defenders look away
pretend they haven't
and now this looks
like insulting false modesty
from the conquering army.

A team who to a man
believe they'd have made pro
if it wasn't for the high school
injury or cerebral
commitment to real ale
in their early twenties.

Even if you score
you never score,
belying the fact there
are seldom no-score draws
here or any slightly-modified
template of here.

Welcome to the universal mudbath.
An unscrewed stud from
the primordial ooze
the only place no-one likes
to admit
they're winning

The Bitter and Twisted Tale of Phil Masinga

Ooh aah Masinga!
This is a chant that never caught on.
Not that anyone really tried.

A man who entered as feted bride,
exited as ugly bridesmaid in
a South Leeds car park

While his imported friend
considered a lesser light
broke that bond of trust implicit,
by being a star -

becoming a Chief while
Phil became a footnote.

Whenever a friend steals my thunder
I think of Phil Masinga.

Whenever I see someone who
never asked to be hyped
not living up to the hype they
never asked for
I think of Phil Masinga.

Possibly all he wanted was to
be the impotent
racial epithet directed at
African people when Leeds
play in the capital

But he could not be that
ultimate dubious badge of honour
bestowed upon the godlike
Anthony Yeboah.

Volleying them in
off the bar
seemingly every week
ensuring future YouTube sensation.

Ooh aah Masinga!

They didn't sing it in Italy either.

A poor goals-to-games ratio there,
but not quite poor enough
to be revered by Italian anarchists
like Luther Blissett,
nom de plume of a thousand
renegade pamphleteers.

Another qualification failure
another dubious honour.

And so it goes:
33 goals in 132 pro appearances.
Inevitable stint in the Gulf.
Inglorious return to England,
with Coventry City,
thwarted by work permit knock-back.

Messy divorce, alimony, near-bankruptcy.

Back to the township where
it all began.

The neighbours swear they hear
him humming to himself:

Ooh aah Masinga!
Ooh aah Masinga!

Sanctions of the FIFA Ethical Committee

The World Cup
has been stripped from Qatar

Offered to
the Seventh Circle of Hell

That will surely teach them
for complaining about the weather

There are four mascots
All horsemen

Merchandised like ponies
for the children

All the stadium builders
are already dead

The other one
has been stripped from Russia

Offered to R'lyeh
Gothic nightmare corpse city

Infrastructure far from conventional,
yet more than playable

Penniless H.P. Lovecraft
called from grave

monitoring corporate sponsors
assuring branding is to liking

Some hack at the back
sings *Three Lions*, nasally.

WC1/EC1

Trainers with suit, mate
but you ain't convinced me
of the athlete within.

Oh no
Boy in booties,
tie, coffee-stuck hands

I am not duped by your
polar bear feet-meets
penguin costume upper.

There are no Olympians
looking like this.
At all.

There are no sprinters
hurdlers, discus-throwers
or modern pentathletes,

but like the javelin's end
you are quite
the prick.

5. ODDS & SODS

Repeat Offender

SECOND REMINDER NOTICE

Our records show that although
a reminder notice was previously
sent to you

Your council tax account
is *again* in arrears
(Emphasis added)

Red Caps and Bold
Can't you see that
50 per cent of this letter
is written in Red Caps *and* Bold

If you do not bring your
Account up to date
You will lose the right to pay
in instalments and

If you lose the right to pay
in instalments
and you do not pay the full balance
Legal action will be taken

The costs of said action
Will be added to your bill

Red Caps *and* Bold
50 per cent of this letter
is written in Red Caps *and* Bold

So it must be clear to you already
Though it's repeated here
For courtesy's sake

That non-payment
Will also result in you
Being dragged naked
In front of the Town Hall
During commuter rush hour

And shot with massive lasers until dead.

Deep Cuts

I think my hair's depressed, she said.
As cute an announcement as it was,
it was not taken particularly seriously
until they crossed Tower Bridge
and it jumped.

Guess Who's

the monkey on my back
chews on the straw
that broke the camel's
back to black to the wall
to the drawing board
as hard as I've tried
attempts to bring sexy back
have been unequivocally
knocked back

Not Bitter

Love don't live here anymore
but I still forward their mail

Perpetual Winter

Late May '14,
another bitter one.
Imaginary frost coats the flooring
of mediocre bar/restaurants.

Small mammals still hibernate
just feet beneath feet.
The seasonal stylus is stuck -
they are wearing woolly hats.

Indoors.

Raspberry Beret

Since the popularisation
of the headgear in song,
May 1985,
not one has since been seen
in a second hand store.

Apathaiku

Some folk write Haiku
To showcase witty wordplay
I rarely bother

The Consultant' Consultant

Don't consult anyone
until you have consulted me.

I am the sole conduit
for the best
non-consultancy related
consultation.

A Consultant Consultant –
Twenty
Months now

A veritable veteran
combatant in the
Consultant Consultancy
arena.

Business booming
management spines flopping
more flaccid than ever

As we all know
leadership has changed
been outsourced, sensibly

Careers of consultants
resting on my pronouncements
Mojito bills paid for, naturally

Opportunity knocks
for the most meta

My expertise expertise
utterly unparalleled

Consulted on all manner
of consultancies
massive to bijou.

So, consultantees:
Don't invest in uncertainty
invest in me.

Then someone else.

Casio MT-20

Plink plonk plink plonk
playing synths 'til fingers ache
'til the hole
where the lead sticks in
breaks.

The realisation,
blotted by drum machine clatter
that a hit was never
on the cards
never ever mattered.

It's the sonic fuzz,
no-one else hears,
that throbbing gristle
hiss and sizzle tinnitus.

This is the calling of the true
bedroom electronicist.

No opening

My key is called
Allen.
Frankly it
suits him.

If my key
Wore a name tag,
it would
Say ALLEN,
Capitalised
Arial size 36
Bold

Underneath,
KEY,
in slightly
smaller font.

Allen is a
pragmatic key
functional
and there's nowt
wrong with that.

Unfortunately
Allen sees himself
more as
a flair player
a Pierre, Juan-Pablo
or even Alain.

But for all
his attempts
at avant-garde
twisting and turning
it's still
reliable, predictable
gets the job
done.

Alas, Allen,
For all his talents,
has yet to come
to terms with
the utter cruelty
of the Universe.

Gold, Frankincense and That

They got Christmas
decorations up early
in the
Payday Loan
Shop
They say
he paid off
Man's debt
by dying
that kid in the
plastic manger by the
small print
but
Twinkle Twinkle
those little stars
have a certain
strobing threat
to them
and I wonder
what you owe

Going Out

And we know this is the end
but it's far from fashionable
to admit it
so we sit on designer sledges,
hoping for a nuclear winter

Left Untitled

The critics,
and the coroner, agreed

That the choked poet's
half-arsed
attempt to swallow
The Complete Works of Milton

on National Poetry Day

was pretty much
as poetic an end
as was probably intended.

Vision of the Future

What would a world
without similes
be like?

Poetic Potential

The small mercies of London town
You should write a poem about that

This documentary I saw on TV last night
You should write a poem about that

The feeling you can't escape a bad flat share
You should write a poem about that

This thing my mum said the other week
(Or maybe it was the week before)
You should write a poem about that

The amount of time you haven't had sex for
You should write a poem about that

The dizzy feeling the docs can't diagnose
You should write a poem about that

The stunted conversations at funerals
You should write a poem about that

The fact the grass is sometimes greener on the other side
You should write a poem about that

All the buzzwords you accidentally started saying
Unironically after beginning ironically
You should write a poem about that

The way the mind goes blank when you score a goal
You should write a poem about that

Your attempt to enjoy these poems is considered unsatisfactory

Your suggestion pessimism is closer to realism
You should write a poem about that

This guy I once met in Ibiza about 2007
You should write a poem about that

When the semblance of a good idea
Goes on for too long
Starts becoming somewhat worse for wear
And eventually more or less caves in on itself
You should write a poem about that

Well there you go - it's done now.

<u>Before they were published here and after they were typed into a massive Word document, some of the pieces appeared elsewhere.</u>

Wheelchair Porn Queen, South Bank Poetry, Inc Zine, Meat Plough - The Journal of Transgressive Poetry, here/there:poetry, Lunar Poetry, 1,000 Monkeys Anthology #2, Surrey Advertiser, The Alarmist, The Morning Star, Crowsfeet, Map zine, 14, The Delinquent, Belleville Park Pages, Poetry Bus, The Keystone Anthology, Evidently: The Anthology, Potluck magazine.

Man and sunbed, Freud's only knock-knock joke, Detail, Enter the Void, The Bitter and Twisted tale of Phil Masinga and *Deep Cuts* were featured in *The Long and the Short of it*, a show performed at the 2012 Edinburgh Fringe alongside Richard Purnell.

Do as Diouf, Lorry on a Narrow Road, Strangers in a Home and *Wednesday, Early Evening* were featured in *Moraletry*, a show performed at the 2013 Edinburgh Fringe, also alongside Richard Purnell.

Your Attempt to Enjoy this Poem is Considered Unsatisfactory, The New English Hymnal, Pessimist's Anthem, Street Soccer Tactics, Entente Cordiale, Field Day, WC1/EC1, Up'nComing, Kingdom in Exile, No Opening and *Vision of the Future* were featured in *Yeti*, Gary's debut solo show, performed at the 2014 Edinburgh Fringe.

Gary From Leeds generally says his poems on stage, but this collection is on paper, because he's a contrary git. On the pages within you can find some examples of high forms of wit, if you're willing to wade through all the low forms. He hopes you enjoy it.

"An oddly charismatic poet with some wonderfully bizarre ideas" - Broadway Baby

"Flow, bite and panache in equal measure" - Nottingham Post

"The blurring between storyteller-style stand-up and comic poetry is hugely entertaining, and for me was an entirely new, very welcome subset of spoken word." - Poetry Monthly

100 Your attempt to enjoy these poems is considered unsatisfactory

102 Your attempt to enjoy these poems is considered unsatisfactory

Lightning Source UK Ltd.
Milton Keynes UK
UKOW02f0213070616

275779UK00002B/37/P